Hi, Duke:
A.M.G.D., I guess.
George Starbuck

BONE THOUGHTS

Volume 56 of the
Yale Series of Younger Poets,
edited by Dudley Fitts
and published on the
Mary Cady Tew Memorial Fund

BONE THOUGHTS

GEORGE STARBUCK

Foreword by Dudley Fitts

New Haven: Yale University Press, 1960

© *1960 by George Starbuck. Set in Monotype Aldine Bembo type and printed in the United States of America by the Printing-Office of the Yale University Press.*

First published, March, 1960

Second printing, April, 1960

Third printing, November, 1961

ACKNOWLEDGMENT is made to the following periodicals for poems originally appearing in them: *The Antioch Review, Audience, Beloit Poetry Journal, Chicago Review, Harper's Magazine, The Humanist, New Campus Writing, The New Republic, The New Yorker, Paris Review, Poetry, Prairie Schooner, Saturday Review, Yale Review.*

"Bone Thoughts on a Dry Day," the second of the "Poems from a First Year in Boston," "Diabolist," "Technologies," "To His Chi Mistress," and "Communication to the City Fathers of Boston," © 1957, 1958, 1959, 1960 by *The New Yorker.*

"Elegy," © 1957 by Bantam Books, Inc.

To the one with her head out the window, drinking the rain.
To the one who said me a lullaby over the phone.
To the one who, divining love in this rocky terrain,
  has made it her own.

FOREWORD

THE BEST INTRODUCTION to a first book of poems is the book
itself. Editorial intervention, however unobtrusive it may be, is
bound to make something of a ceremony out of what should be
a natural event; and a good poet needs no Master of Ceremonies.
Nevertheless, the circumstances of a first formal appearance may
be such as to justify a word or two of comment *ab extra*; and the
idea of the Yale Series of Younger Poets, involving annual com-
petition and judgment, provides me with an excuse for doing
what I should have wanted to do in any event—prologuizing,
briefly, in the Euripidean manner. Obviously my regard for Mr.
Starbuck's work is high: by recommending his book for publi-
cation I have testified to that much. The special nature of the
occasion calls for some sort of public accounting, an explanation
of what it was in this manuscript that prompted me to act as I did.

Accident, of course, plays a part in any such decision as this.
There are various ways into a new book. It may be an idea that
catches the imagination, or an image, or some happy trick of
phrasing. It was a stylistic flourish, an instance of technical
bravura, that first interested me in Mr. Starbuck's poems. Read-
ing at random, I was arrested by what seemed to me an extraor-
dinarily handsome complication of sights and noises:

> Full-feasted
> Spring, like an ill bird, settles to the masthead
> of here and there an elm. The streets are misted.
> A Boston rain, archaic and monastic,
> cobbles the blacktop waters, brings mosaic
> to dusty windshields; to the waking, music.

An intricate and charming sound. The first triad of assonances
moving from bright to dull, the second from dull to bright; the
varying incidence of the caesura, imposing a new melody upon
the already counterpointed basic line; the resolution in a *clausula*

—"to the waking, music"—reflecting the movement of the whole passage: this was admirable composition, even if one stopped with the technic. Was there anything more than the technic? What lay behind the sound? A great deal, I thought; enough, at any rate, to expand this prose corner of Boston into a mechanistic metropolitan Everywhere. The instant of bare trees, cars parked overnight, wet sidewalks, open bedroom windows—this comprehends a world of dejection and renewal, of despair and ("mosaic / to dusty windshields; to the waking, music") hope. The perception is total, thoroughly realized in the working out. The passage challenges the ear, it engages the mind, it fills the imagination. My own predilections being what they are, I entered it through the gate of sound; but that is idiosyncratic and unimportant. Wherever one enters, the structure here is composed and complete.

"Composed" is not a fashionable word. Much of the new poetry, to judge from my own editorial experience, is warily, even wearily, formal; but there is little evidence that composition, the painfully thought-through building of verse, is held in honor, or even very well understood. The failures of my own generation took refuge in the disintegrating eccentricities of Dada and post-Dada, which gave them at least a spurious kind of vivacity; the failures of today seem to head for whatever abandoned shelter of formalism is available to them and squat there in the discomfortable gloom. Here is no question of a choice between freedom and restraint, for that can be an intelligent choice. Here, too often, there is no artistic intelligence at work, or only enough of it to grasp pathetically at a poetic form—a stanza, a syntax, an imagery, a vocabulary—without bothering, or even wanting, to make the structure one's own, to reapply and rebuild. Hence the depressing spectacle of young traditionalists too untaught, or too obtuse, to understand the traditions that they assert. Hence a great deal of inert verse; but hence, too, the shock of refreshment that one takes from the work of a man who makes his own forms, by and large, composing them passionately and learnedly from the ground up.

I was also attracted, and sometimes repelled, by Mr. Starbuck's wit. Here I am on shakier ground, since one may see a smile where someone else sees only a grin or a grimace: *de risu non est disputandum*. Certainly there are escapades in these poems, some of them more spontaneous than others, that fade rather quickly once their point has been made. Mr. Starbuck could use an intellectual sedative. Most often, however, his wit is the serious wit that is the energizing ally of tragic poetry. I find a brutally specific example of what I mean in the jukebox rancor of "War Story":

> The 4th of July he stormed a nest.
> He won a ribbon but lost his chest.
> We threw his arms across the rest
>   And kneed him in the chin.
>   (You knee them in the chin
>   To drive the dog-tag in.)

At first sight this looks like an easy playing for shock; but if you consider the second and third lines more attentively, you will see that it is not. The joking is scabrous, like the occasion that gives rise to it; but it is stiffened and controlled by an accurate handling of antithesis and paradox, and it is this queer rigor that discovers the pity in the horror. This is the saving violence of wit, and it is to be contrasted with a merely cynical effect occurring later in the same poem, where

> The widow lay on her davenport
>   Letting the news sink in.
>   (Since April she had been
>   Letting the news sink in.)

Here the shock, released by that second syzygy of *s*'s, is aimed rather at the guts than at the head. But even this joke, if you call it a joke, has its place in the economy of the poem. It is right, somehow, even in its wrongness; and it is because Mr. Starbuck's wit is usually right, artistically and philosophically, that I cite it as one of attractive qualities of his work. Someone is sure to object that I am now talking about "light verse," whatever that may be. Very possibly I am; but if "War Story" and the other rimed poems in this manner are "light verse," they are also an intense and shaking kind of poetry, an art whose dissonances and wry dartings reflect a man awake in the nightmare of our day. It is the dusty windshield again; but it is also the gleam of mosaic.

Such, at any rate, was my first encounter with this manuscript. I shall say nothing about the longer poems, except that they seem to me—particularly the Boston pieces—exact and proper in their disdain and deeply moving in their bewildered tenderness. Nor shall I attempt a museum tour of the epigrammatic poems, the latent and overt *jeux d'esprit,* the verses that are fun for the sake of fun. What I have said here is a prelude to a prelude, and it would be impertinent to try for a conclusion. A first book of poems may be no more than an overture, but it is also no less. To my mind, all the evidence suggests that a great song is begun.

DUDLEY FITTS

CONTENTS

PART ONE: CREATURES

BONE THOUGHTS ON A DRY DAY

Walking to the museum
over the Outer Drive,
I think, before I see them
dead, of the bones alive.

How perfectly the snake smoothes over the fact
he strings sharp beads around that charmer's neck.

Bird bone may be breakable, but
have you ever held a cat's jaw shut?
Brittle as ice.

Take mice:
the mouse is a berry, his bones mere seeds:
step on him once and see.

You mustn't think that the fish
choke on those bones, or that chickens wish.

The wise old bat
hangs his bones in a bag.

Two chicks ride a bike,
unlike
that legless swinger of crutches, the ostrich.

Only the skull of a man is much of an ashtray.

Each owl
turns on a dowel.

When all the other tents are struck, an old
elephant pitches himself on his own poles.

But as for my bones—
tug of a toe, blunt-bowed barge of a thighbone,
gondola-squadron of ribs, and the jaw scow—
they weather the swing and storm of the flesh they plow,
out of conjecture of shore, one jolt from land.

I climb the museum steps like a beach.
There, on squared stone, some cast-up keels bleach.
Here, a dark sea speaks with white hands.

NEW STRAIN

You should see these musical mice.
　　When we start the device
they rise on their haunches and sniff
　　the air as if
they remembered all about dancing.
　　Soon they are chancing
a step or two, and a turn.
　　How quickly they learn
the rest, and with leaps and spins
　　master the ins
and outs of it, round and round
　　and round. We found
the loudest music best
　　and now we test
with a kind of electric bell
　　which works as well.

In two to two-and-a-quarter
　　minutes, a shorter
rhythm captures the front
　　legs, and they stunt
in somersaults until
　　they become still
and seem to have lost their breath.
　　But the sign of death
is later: the ears, which have been
　　flat, like a skin
skullcap, relax and flare
　　as if the air
might hold some further thing
　　for the listening.

FABLE FOR BLACKBOARD

Here is the grackle, people.
Here is the fox, folks.
The grackle sits in the bracken. The fox
    hopes.

Here are the fronds, friends,
that cover the fox.
The fronds get in a frenzy. The grackle
    looks.

Here are the ticks, tykes,
that live in the leaves, loves.
The fox is confounded,
and God is above.

FABLE FOR FLIPPED LID

There was a rat
who, whatever
he did, never
stopped getting fat-
ter and fatter fast-
er and faster till at last . . .

but I mustn't get
ahead of my story.
The laboratory
had to keep set-

ting him tougher and tough-
er problems . . . ENOUGH!
I must be chron-
ological.
One. They all
had to run

mazes. Two.
When they got through

a maze the prize
was food. Thirdly,
the more hurriedly,
the more size-

able. Fourthly, the more
. . . What was four?
Listen, I ran
this lab, and it wasn't
so very pleasant
having him an-

swer the questions quick
as the staff could pick

them out of the dic-
tionary IT MAKES ME SICK

all this bother about who
ate up the Grant.
I asked him "Well can't
you stop?" "Dunno how to,"

he said, "I hate
being overweight,

but in the heat
of competition
I've no volition:
I just compete.

I get carried away.
I'd eat Cape May

if I won it." I would-
n't put it past him.
One day I asked him
if he was so good

why didn't he
go on TV

and make a hundred
and sixty-four
grand, and what's more,
he did. I wondered

where it would lead to,
but I didn't need to:

he choked on a room-
ful of non-retur-
nable furniture
from "Bride and Groom."

ONE MAN'S GOOSE; OR, POETRY REDEFINED

I

One of the most quoted *ko-an* of the Zen Buddhists goes as follows: *There is a live goose in a bottle. How does one remove the goose without hurting it or damaging the bottle?* An admired answer is "Behold, I have done it!" There is a definition of poetry to be found in this. John Holmes (*Saturday Review,* March 1, 1958) found it. His poem ends:

> I put it in with my words.
> I took it out the same way.
> And what worked with these
> Can work with any words I say.

2

I had a lovely bottle, bottle-blue
in color with a heavy bottle-shape.
It filled my kitchen table (window too)
as round, as fine, as dusty as a grape,
but not as edible.

                Reading my friend
John Holmes's poem "Poetry Defined;
or a Short Course in Goose-Bottling by Mind-
Over-Matter," I smiled: I saw an end
to certain problems. Yes, a goose would serve.

Laying out axe and pot, steeling my nerve,
"Doggone, I've put this goose in this-here bottle,"
I said. And it worked: there she was—a beaut! all
white and afraid. Now:

                "There she is!" I cried.
Thunk went the fatted shoulders. Well, she tried.
"There she is!" *Thunk*. "THERE she is!"

                      What the heck,
they came out, goose and bottle, neck and neck
each time. Seizing the pot-lid, *Thwack!* My eyes
buzzed as the blue-green bits like sizzling flies
diamond-drilled them. Oh, if words could show them:
fires, flares, rockets, the works! *There* was a poem!
(spent like a wish, of course, after one use)

but here, Kind Reader, here is our bruised goose.

AB OVO

Beak gumming my entrails,
wings elbowing my temples,
there's this bird wants out.

Suppose I just let crack,
and he rolls out the red neck,
where would you put your foot?

If he bows a backward knee,
if he stands there woodenly,
is this a dove, or what?

Lady, he may be moist,
liquid-tongued, not voiced,
with wattles on his throat.

Lady, in a word,
this fabled headlong bird
Love is a strange coot.

DIABOLIST

Through water his own waterfall
furthering, the electric eel
loops downward into a drowned pool
of himself. Snowfall and storm coil
to the same fold, invisible
as sleep. He is their shepherd. Whole

oceans above him turn and spool
silver from valleys. A slow wheel
tears you from me, Love—beautiful
as the sea. And when your eyes, all
depth and breadth of the world we fell,
brim, do I flicker there like coal?

TECHNOLOGIES

On Commonwealth, on Marlborough,
the gull beaks of magnolia
were straining upward like the flocks
harnessed by kings in storybooks
who lusted for the moon. Six days
we mooned into each other's eyes
mythologies of dune and dawn—
naked to the Atlantic sun,
loving and loving, to and fro
on Commonwealth, on Marlborough,
our whole half-hours. And where our bloods
crested, we saw the bruise-red buds
tear loose the white, impeded shapes
of cries. And when our whitest hopes
tore at the wind with wings, it seemed
only a loony dream we dreamed,
such heavy machination of
cars and motels confronted love
on Commonwealth, on Marlborough.
They do the trick with rockets now—
with methodologies of steel—
with industry or not at all.
But so, sweet love, do these white trees
that dare play out their lunacies
for all they are, for all they know
on Commonwealth, on Marlborough.

PART TWO: STRUCTURES

TO HIS CHI MISTRESS

I

It's spring: the City, wrapped
in unaccustomed grace,
goes scarlet where they slapped
a garden in her face
right in the sunken place
she found her rotten set
of ivory towers gapped
when the last fair pulled out.

We head out for the park
from Iris and Rose's bar.
Watching the dancers bare
their little almost-all,
letting the whiskey work,
lusty and lachrymal,
has primed us: it's not far:
it might as well befall.

II

The elms along the drag,
so mop and yet so fag—
these pigeon-breasted hags
with their nobby arms awag
climactically above
a congregation of
iris and roses, Love—
have shaken off their doves.

Bare ruined chorus-lines,
for what they are, they stand.
The winos give them a hand.

Where amber light refines
our company of flowers
to wax, it may be hours
before some bluecoat shines
his hunger onto ours.

III

Well we didn't come to Walt's,
we didn't come to Dan's,
we come to Rose and Iris's,
Iris's, man.

Their shapes may be piracies,
their colors may be false,
but you know you've seen a dance
when they shake that schmaltz.

IV

Winds of morning sift
down through the heavy wires
and branches like a gift
of tongues. Our voices drift
lazily on a wash
of motors, brushes, tires—
street-cleaning—the soft flush
of a cat-house after hours.

We'll make it: worlds of time:
even the winos seem
posted to see us home;
and shoring up the elms,
shoring up the el,
lighting up an L & M
butt, they serve as well
as any sentinel.

V

Behind us, the gates lock.
The iron rolling-stock
of the bankrupt CTA
jolts, and gets underway.
This is the only Rock:
give with your knees, and sway
close to the very wreck
they had here yesterday.

Back of the yellowed laces
flaunting past our faces,
dispirited embraces
yellow bed after bed.
With some who will curse bread,
with some who will free races,
the sooty slut replaces
her defeated dead.

COMMUNICATION TO THE CITY FATHERS OF BOSTON

Dear Sirs: Is it not time we formed a Boston
Committee to Enact a Dirge for Boston?

When New York mushrooms into view, when Boston's
townspeople, gathered solemnly in basements,
feel on their necks the spiderwebs of bombsights,
when subway stations clot and fill like beesnests
making a honey-heavy moan, whose business
will it be then to mourn, to take a busman's
holiday from his death, to weep for Boston's?

Though dust is scattered to her bones, though grieving
thunderheads add hot tears, though copper grapevines
clickety-clack their telegraphic ragtime
tongues at the pity of it, how in God's name
will Boston in the thick of Armageddon
summon composure to compose a grave-song
grave and austere enough for such a grieving?

Move we commit some song, now, to the HOLD files
of papers in exotic places. Helpful
of course to cram our scholars with hogs' headfuls
of Lowells, khaki-cap them, ship them wholesale
to Wake or Thule—some safe base, where heartfelt
terror may milk them of a tear; but Hell's fire,
what'll they have on us in all those HOLD files?

You want some rewrite man to wrap up Boston
like garbage in old newsprint for the dustbin?
The Statehouse men convivial at Blinstrub's,
the textile men, the men of subtler substance
squiring Ledaean daughters to the swan-boats,
the dockers, truckers, teen-age hotrod-bandits—
what could he make of them, to make them Boston?

Or even make of me, perched in these Park Street
offices playing Jonah like an upstart
pipsqueak in raven's clothing—First Mate Starbuck
who thinks too much? Thinking of kids in bookstores
digging for dirty footnotes to their Shakespeares,
while by my window the Archbishop's upstairs
loudspeaker booms redemption over Park Street.

Thinking of up the hill the gilded Statehouse
where just last night the plaster-of-paris faces
of Sacco and Vanzetti craned on flannel
arms at the conscientiously empaneled
pain of a state's relentlessly belated
questioning of itself. (Last year the Salem
Witches; next year, if next year finds a Statehouse . . . ?)

Thinking of Thor, Zeus, Atlas. Thinking Boston.
Thinking there must be words her weathered brownstone
could still re-whisper—words to blast the brassbound
brandishers on their pads—words John Jay Chapman
scored on her singlehanded—words Sam Adams,
Garrison, Mott, Thoreau blazed in this has-been
Braintree-Jamaica-Concord-Cambridge-Boston.

There were such men. Or why remember Boston?
Strange how not one prepared a dirge for Boston.

April, 1959

WORSHIP

Lofting fungoes at the rose
window of a church of elms,
evening worshipers with bat and ball
praise beyond idolatry that force
they, their symbols, and their act embody.
Morning worshipers with cap and shawl
bodied forth in off-to-market Fords
bump and haggle down the same
never-desecrated aisles.

Noon is lone: its worshiper
feels his chapel of gray flesh
lit and musicked by the jewelled elms
telling sun across his helpless hands.
Sunday all break worship, knock to church
grave as guilt can grin, to try stiff thoughts
on ungainly wood or word, and all,
feeling virtue leave them, cry
mea culpa, but sit tight.

PROGNOSIS

Petrarch watched a plague: it took
half of Europe, says my book.
Now of course we've found the rat.
Anyway, half lived. And yet

something very like a plague
propagates, and while our vague
fears breed fear, the insecure
vaccinate themselves—with fear.

Flesh, that to uranium
seems a power vacuum,
cannot linger uncommitted:
sooner, later, all are pitted.

Saved from Mao and Molotov,
millions leave the clinic of
Doctor Dulles, Doctor Nixon,
rabid with their antitoxin.

Millions more, on Khrushchev's serum,
rage with fear of those that fear them.
Shadows prowl at every back.
All precaution is attack.

Still, the books will skimp it, if
here and there a spasm of life
raises on the ruins one
knowing cross of bone on bone.

Schoolboy Chaucer feared the bog,
fled from shapes of mist and fog.
We can grin, and blame the flea:
air, we know, kills boundlessly.

IF SATURDAY

Four easy hours from San Francisco, yes
the sitting mallards tip like steel-plate ducks.
Among them, clay-pipe fishes leap and pop
before your eyes, before your eyes are there.
As advertised, these mountains cool their claws
and show their sleepless nerves merely as trees:
no crossed gray crosses scratch against the sky.
A frequency of birds pick out a channel,
make their plain statement, fade it into blue.
Lay out your arms like rods on the calm water,
clench and extend your tackle, float it gently
above green fish that measurelessly tread
the green plush colonnades of an obscure
courtiership. Your marriage is this moment.
Great arcs of pine and geese complete your sphere.

Two easy voices and a boat from now,
this soon the evening Limited of wind
at distant crossings laying dismal sounds,
the sun comes to your level like a friend.
Dying a friend, it leaks away, unhurried
as a man of time . . . But what upstart humps
in with a sun grin at the deathbed's left—
what idiot Announcer—what Late Flash?
whose ripe orange orb of power, risen, rots—
holes in your eyes too deep, too black for water.
The bomb. Who would have thought. The bomb. But there
the bastions rise until the capstone's on
that tipping monolith of cloud; and now
as ever a south-flying mallard swings
like any late commuter to the moving
platform of the warping, wooden water.

The trees fall singly into dark formation.
You, with your untried gun, inherit all.
Down in the valleys, dust rain will be falling
and leaning masts above suburban dwellings
claw empty pictures from the breeding air.
And you, with your lines dry, inherit all.
Row to the shore. The bomb. The bomb, the bastards.
Tell it, the two of you. Say until morning.
Say till the world retakes its age-old shapes,
lifting again the green receiving branches
eight easy minutes from the sun. The roads
will have their fill awhile of flesh in motion,
mindlessly nerved to murder as it dies.
Nations convulsing, their great thought gone static,
try your mere voices; try small work of hands.
One must begin by helping one; and you,
best-armed of pioneers, most learned savage,
granted a day's north wind, inherit all.

THREE DREAMS ON A WARM SABBATH

I

The heavy-breasted Persian rugs
contain their breathing.
The royal Pictish writing desk
stops heaving.
Brown Indian inkwells raise
their lacerated cups of palm in praise.
Abstracted, while the full wells spill,
he sucks his quill.

Or dips, and writes, and dips and writes until
papyrus blooms
and it is April
splattering buds in the woman-heated room.

But soot falls thicker on our psalmodist;
another fingerabrum gutters at the wrist.
Light ho! Is there no gentle Christian here?
Fresh hands are moved to prayer.

Fresh fingers break the living light
unequally among the black, the white,
the brown tonalities, but all are blest.

And Nero, gaunt with metric balancing—
Nero with heedless hardon slumbering—
strides to the forum, robed in eyes aghast,
stills the ovation, and begins to sing.

II

Here is the peak of pressure, here of heat,
here the descending tension in the feet,
and here we have the computed muscle-tone.

The moment, you notice, passes and is gone,
and if the observer's eye should blink, is lost;
but with the polygraph, five colored lines
preserve the entire sequence, and refine
the sensitivity, while cutting costs.

Nero, she thinks, poor fumbler of a poet.
But drowns her daydream in her work again,
an idiosyncratic nobbed white pen
bundled with four fat fingers, going to it.

Color of lemon leaves, the tasteful chambers
are lit by one orange lamp of curious shade.
The shadow heart in blue and red that clambers
from wall to wall like a negative ship's beacon
lurches unhealthily. Like carpets beaten,
a dusty noise: the Brits: another raid.

Thrown to the warm night air, her window passes
strange soot that swirls to clothe the naked shade.
She dreams a starched white coat, attentive classes,
complaint of small routine that saps her days,
and questions answered with abstracted gaze
in a chaste office on the south arcade.

Which brings the Bitch of Buchenwald to tears.
Head back, she lets them dazzle to the kick
of gunfire. Searchlights writhe. Percussion nears.
She pirouettes in kliegs of Q.E.D.
Her swivelchair winds down, and crazily
across the ceiling sprawls *ich liebe dich.*

III

The sunlight presses against the ordinary window.
A child kicks me as if I were his.
My hand poises with a yellow wooden pencil
over the page.

Under my smudges of lead, crossed-out lines:
Their blood—their sputtering blood—marrows that whine—
Matter of taste, taste.
And worse:
Unstoppering a song—
So much I could write is wrong.

Son, flesh of my flesh—ah, pounds—
what am I hiding, a few indelicate sounds?
Angel of accident, caught in the sun,
over your blondness a dust-mote
riding on angry atoms
bounds and rebounds.

Tapping my foolscap, counting time
for Taiwan, Budapest, Madrid, South Boston,
fists of a million salaried enforcers
balancing my repose, I twinkle rhymes.

A TAPESTRY FOR BAYEUX

I. *Recto*

Over the
  seaworthy
cavalry
  arches a
rocketry
  wickerwork:
involute
  laceries
lacerate
  indigo
altitudes,
  making a
skywritten

filigree
  into which,
lazily,
  LCTs
sinuate,
  adjutants
next to them
  eversharp-
eyed, among
  delicate
battleship
  umbrages
twinkling an

anger as
  measured as
organdy.

Normandy
knitted the
   eyelets and
yarn of these
   warriors'
armoring—
   ringbolt and
dungaree,
   cable and
axletree,

tanktrack and
   ammobelt
linking and
   opening
garlands and
   islands of
seafoam and
   sergeantry.
Opulent
   fretwork: on
turquoise and
   emerald,
red instants

accenting
   neatly a
dearth of red.
   Gunstations
issue it;
   vaportrails
ease into
   smoke from it—
yellow and
   ochre and
umber and

  sable and
out. Or that

man at the
 edge of the
tapestry
 holding his
inches of
 niggardly
ground and his
 trumpery
order of
 red and his
equipage
 angled and
dated. He.

II. *Verso*

Wasting no
 energy,
Time, the old
 registrar,
evenly
 adds to his
scrolls, rolling
 up in them
rampage and
 echo and
hush—in each
 influx of
surf, in each

tumble of
 raincloud at
evening,
 action of

seaswell and
  undertow
rounding an
  introvert
edge to the
  surge until,
manhandled
  over, all
surfaces,

tapestries,
  entities
veer from the
  eye like those
rings of lost
  yesteryears
pooled in the
  oak of your
memory.
  Item: one
Normandy
  Exercise.
Muscle it

over: an
  underside
rises: a
  raggedy
elegant
  mess of an
abstract: a
  rip-out of
kidstuff and
  switchboards, where
amputee
  radio
elements,

unattached
  nervefibre
conduits,
  openmouthed
ureters,
  tag ends of
hamstring and
  outrigging
ripped from their
  unions and
nexuses
  jumble with
undeterred

speakingtubes
  twittering
orders as
  random and
angry as
  ddt'd
hornets. Step
  over a
moment: peer
  in through this
nutshell of
  eyeball and
man your gun.

TO JONATHAN EDWARDS, d. 1758

1. *New Year: View West Over Storrow*

Boston. Lord God, the ocean never to windward,
never the sweet snootful of death a West Coast
wind on its seven-league sea-legs winds its wing-ding
landfalling up by upheaving over you.

                    Wonders.
Streetsful of San Francisco my thirst still wanders.
Head still heavy with harvests of rot winrowed
on beaches, hands with a haul of fishes weed-wound
in jetsam of nets, throat with a rise of white-winged
wallowing sea birds, I dream that city, the once-loved
weight of those seas, and the sea-sucked girl I waylayed
through deserts who sours here, a sick wife.

                        With land wind.
Nothing but land wind hot with steel, but lint-white
bundles of daily breath hung out over textile
towns, but the sweat sucked from mines, but white smokestacks
soaring from hospital workyards over grassplots
of pottering dotards. Life. Life, the wind whispers;
crouch to its weight: three thousand miles, three hundreds-
of-years of life rolled up in a wind, rolled backwards
onto this city's back, Jonathan Edwards.

And never the full sea wind. Lord God, what wonder
kids go skinny and pale as ale down one-way
pavements to pitch pinched pennies onto the subway's
eyes, his cast-iron eyes.

                  Jonathan Edwards,
funny old crank of Social History lectures,
firm believer in hell and witches, who knows whether
you of all witnesses wouldn't watch this wayward
city with most love?

Jonathan, while prim Winter
bustles with steam and batting, bundling the wind-torn
birth of your death's two-hundredth year—while internes,
sober as bloody judges, clean the downtown
haul of the mercy-fleet—while rearing and sounding
through panicked traffic the sacred scows come horns-down
and huge with woe—while heavy-headed thousands
of bells nod off to sleep like practiced husbands
propped in high corners of their lady Boston's
white-laid and darkened room—while worst- and best-born,
Beacon and Charlestown, clench, giving this stubborn
year nineteen hundred fifty-eight its birth-bath
of blood, I turn to you as to a sabbath—
turn, as the drugged dawn deadens, to the solace
of your staid rage.
           At least no wretch went soulless
when you had damned him Man. Nor would you sell us
that Freedom-to-end-Freedoms that the self-sold
crow about: Freedom from Guilt, they name it, shiftless
for any other shrift. Yachtsmen, their footloose
legatees fitting reefers into faultless
features with febrile wrists, protest: some leftist
restlessness threatens them in brittle leaflets;
some angry boy, some undiscovered artist
has put soot whiskers on their public statues.
They wring their strange left hands that every-whichways
scatter the khakied corpses onto elsewhere's
turbulent waters to save oil. The world-wise
rage at the world—
           where you, Jonathan Edwards,
wise to the same sad racket, bore some inward
wisdom, some inward rage. There and there only,
letting this city sicken me and own me,
knowing the grief there is, taking it on me,
may I hope (having not your Christ for bondsman)
to earn these hearts, their paradise, this Boston.

11. *Outbreak of Spring*

Stirring porchpots up with green-fingered witchcraft,
insinuating cats in proper outskirts,
hag Spring in a wink blacks the prim white magic
of winter-wimpled Boston's every matesick
splinter of spinster landscape.
      Under the matchstick
march of her bridgework, melting, old lady Mystic
twitches her sequins coyly, but the calls
of her small tugs entice no geese. Canals
take freight; the roads throw up stiff hands, and the Charles
arches. Spring's ón us: a life raft wakes the waters
of Walden like a butt-slap.
      And yet she loiters.
Where is song while the lark in winter quarters
lolls? What's to solace Scollay's hashhouse floaters
and sing them to their dolls? and yet—
       strange musics,
migrant melodies of exotic ozarks,
twitter and throb where the bubble-throated jukebox
lurks iridescent by these lurid newsracks.
Browser leafing here, withhold your wisecracks:
tonight, in public, straight from overseas,
her garish chiaroscuro turned to please
you and her other newsstand devotees,
the quarter-lit Diana takes her ease.

So watch your pockets, cats, hang onto your hearts,
for when you've drunk her glitter till it hurts—
Curtain.
    Winds frisk you to the bone.
       Full-feasted
Spring, like an ill bird, settles to the masthead
of here and there an elm. The streets are misted.
A Boston rain, archaic and monastic,
cobbles the blacktop waters, brings mosaic
to dusty windshields; to the waking, music.

III. *Surfeit and Hot Sleep*

Heavy on branch, on tight green knuckles heaves
the Spring. Cumulus, thick as broodhens, thieves
green from the earthy bark like worms, like leaves,
like dollars from up sleeves.
                              Outbreak of billfolds,
bellbottoms, burleycue babes. Musical billboards
join the parade. And deep in bars the railbirds
listen: "They selling something?" "Can't tell, traffic."
On corners cats bounce once or twice: "Hey frantic."
"Yeah." and they stop. Flared forward like an intake
the lips lurch on. DISASTER OUTLET, NATICK
BEHEMOTH BARGAINS MONSTER DEALS TITANIC
the soundtruck reads; but what it says is "Mine.
You're my obsession. No I can't resign
possession. I'm confessin' that you're mine
mine mine mine mine click." Da Capo. Move on.

Slowly the moon, that shifty chaperone,
performs her preconcerted wink, but none
are quite prepared. Hag Spring's had it: she's made
her bed of faggots and goes up in jade
flame like the tough old bird she is. Green, green
upon green, hips the store windows—I mean
it's summer now, that lolloping large mother,
comes puttering about some spell or other
among her brats the beasts.
                              But back streets trammel
her traipse with tracks and snood her up in metal;
she smiles from Fenway's temple walls too madly
to matter much, and though admission's free,
few worship, fewer dance, and none with glee.

What then? Her bouncing boy—that honeyed wonder's
hernia'd ruiner Love—has aged no tenderer:
portly he paces the parks, poking under
odd scraps of news his forcible reminder
what buds had best be at. They mull it over.

Rest, Mr. Edwards, not a Boston voter
calls him paisan: save your grave pocket veto;
for if they still make time in Waltham's drugstores,
if ladies see new light on Beacon's backstairs,
the fault's not Venus's, it's not the Dog Star's;
if Cupid's in, he's not the deepest prankster;
for spring and fall and all, the hapless hustler
cries her undoubted wound in rouge past picture
palaces; winter long her helter-skelter
sisters go squealing to the marriage-smelter:
the tin-pan Moon, the Moon's to blame!
                                        for throngs
follow the bouncing ball and sing along,
"Moon, salivary Moon, won't you please be
around, Moon, silv'ry dollar Moon so's we
can go to town, Moon: ain' no one aroun'
to get us high, O, Dionysian Moon,
like to die . . ." Moon. Lubricious spinster. Crone.
A pox!—
            Powder with stardust. And the bride's
the broad's the broodmare's Moon at a cloud's side
poses, while slowly the light is hers. She glides,
golden, an apple of eyes, and so cold, only
heart at its heaviest can join the lonely
circle in emptiness that is her dance.
Yet she is Love, our Love, that frantic cadence.
Listen:
        O Love, Love, but I had such dreams!
The wood was thick but knived with light, and streams
from a warm spring tangled about my feet.
Behind me the single pair of hooves beat
and shaggy hands played in the splash of my heels.
"Sister!" I cried, "Diana . . ."   and the squeals
of the magpie bushes, ricochet of stones
struck from his hooves like sparks, impertinence
of woodmice in the leaves, and all sound, stopped.

Far and treeless away the gray plain steeped
to blackness. I leapt far—but slow, through heavy
moonlight, so slow in a long falling the very
land seemed to cringe from me, and that blue moon
—Earth—to reach out for me— (O Love be bone,
be burning flesh, be weight and heat and breath,
bear me beneath your bodysweight of earth
to earth) I woke and dreamed I was alone.

Crying. Poor creatures tying across the torn
spilt-milk grin of a sheet their sweating knot—
while at the westward window see with what
aplomb the round haunch of the Moon hangs through,
and far back in the dark she truckles to,
stoppling her champagne giggles, what dark crew . . .

IV. *Autumn: Progress Report*

Becalmed in old Back Bay's dead water sulk
the square four-storey barges, hulk to hulk.
These increments, so brusquely set aside
by the busy longshore muscle of the tide,
nurse the cut glint of chandelier and cup
like geodes: here Cathay lies silted up,
where tides of trade once moved: old weather eyes
look from the mansard portholes sans surmise.
Sans tooth, sans claw, late blood-competitors
hold in the faces of inheritors
a tight precarious old man's embrace.

Whaddaya do for action in this place?
Taxicabs scuttle by on the wet streets.
I weave with two sweet ladies out of the Ritz,
stare at the Garden pond.
                              Old pioneer,
Jonathan Edwards, did you stop off here
where marsh birds skittered, and a longboat put
its weed-grown bones to pasture at the foot
of Beacon, close on Charles Street? And see then,
already sick with glut, this hill of men?
And even there, see God? And in this marsh,
and in the wood beyond, grace of a harsh
God? And in these crabbed streets, unto the mid-
mire of them, God? Old Soul, you said you did.

It's still the same congested spit of land—
Dry Heaven's devil's-island, where the banned
gods of the blood's regime still play at court
in the stripped palatial prisons of the heart.
Poor pagan spooks, so gently spoken of
in Boston—brainwashed beggar-ghosts of love
so painfully, as if we knew such gods,
trying our neoclassical façades—

Prayer without praise. Glut in the atrium.

Jonathan, praise may be when the heart's drum
carries from camp to camp through jungles of
an entwined dark flesh, and the beat of love,
forcing that forest, overflows the sky.

Vegetal flesh, huge-bosomed, fills the eye
on Washington Street. Portly drummers croak,
their clotted hearts into their hands, no joke,
unsounded and unsung. You had your grand
God at your heart—could tremble in his hand—
could stare the cold stars through and find his voice
cupped in your ear by farthest space: "Rejoice
that you know not!"—could know, curled by God's spit
in dust, his meanest Incarnation: it
can be State Street and Monday Noon: it may
be drunk as a Lord: a guy might well say
"Christ!" scooting by.
                              And Christ why bleed about
some Kingdom we can never know, cast out
with all our flesh and blood before our birth?
Why not take stock of this stone island, earth,
and dig for its downed gods? Christ I could laugh,
so many pray; and yet—
                              I have seen half
the sculpted heads of Boston make the face
of one caged lion of a man their place
of weary battle: every day again
he must survive them all—the lettered men,
the men of means, the men of parts and shares—
and if he seeks God's peace instead of theirs,
God rest him for it: though I no more can
stomach your God than you my faith in man,
I too must worship blindly, Jonathan.

PART THREE: HIGHER CREATURES

"AMONG THOSE KNOWN
TO HAVE BEEN SUSPECTED
IN THIS CONNECTION..."

They hold a committee today.
They hold it over me.
I wasn't invited. They say
the public gets in free.

The man I have this from
wouldn't divulge his face.
I heard, in the dead hum
that took his voice's place,

something I almost hear
in you. (You purse your eyes,
look from ear to ear
and back again.) Surmise

a room, the table set
with fists, the fists with sheaves
of evidence as yet
safe in manila sleeves.

Suppose commercials done,
cameras, papers, fists
set moving, everyone
plunged in light to the wrists.

Say, when those hands aghast,
those thumbs awag with woe,
jig like the naked cast
of a Punch and Judy show,

that pretty comedy
draws millions. Say they gawk
too openmouthed for glee,
too tranquilized for shock.

Say every well-fed gut
unshaken at that jape
eases or freezes shut
one stronghold of escape

and every head that smiles
in torpor or assent
nods me the footloose miles
of my imprisonment . . .

Or say I stood here still,
 waiting for you to speak?
Could I be such a pill?
Have I no friends to seek?

UNFRIENDLY WITNESS

I never played the Moor,
I never looked to see,
I don't know what my hands are for,
I know they're not for me:

I lent them to my Mother,
She yanked them into rules
and put them with my pencilbox
as fit to take to school;

I lent them to my Teacher,
she ruled them into pens
and sent them home to Fatherdear
who beat them straight again;

I lent them to my Judge,
he penned them into line,
since when they clasp and hold I swear
nothing of yours, or mine;

I lent them to my Sergeant,
he lined them into squads
and marched them off to sudden death
like little piston rods;

Death sent them back unused,
I squandered them on love:
they took the world for comrade then
as easy as a glove.

And yet the world is heavy
and filled with men like me—
with tired men, with heavy men
that slip my memory
if that be perjury.

CAPE COD AUTUMN

Deep as Manhattan's earth the billion-dollar
roots of our affluence pull back their saps:
this limb of land grows colder, sheds its colors,
spins from its leeward beaches the bright-veined maps,
goes white— dreaming of next year's green perhaps.
And road maps, reminders, leaflets skim where a sea
of swimmers' ghosts in whiter-than-bathing caps
jostle and duck and leap, where squeals of glee
follow a seagull away, away with their eyes from me.

I sit alone in a jacket and jeans on a dune,
dig in my toes for warmth, and warm the air
in my hands, breathing again that stretch of June
when everything fills, and fills, like a nightmare—
I grin: this is no season of despair:
many a man's banked him a bundle; and hey!
down the horizon it hopped with the four-square
jounce of a full Good Humor, an ice-gray
box of a truck from Brinks Inc hustles the green away.

ON FIRST LOOKING IN ON
BLODGETT'S *KEATS'S "CHAPMAN'S*
HOMER" (*Sum.* ½C. M9–11)

Mellifluous as bees, these brittle men
droning of Honeyed Homer give me hives.
I scratch, yawn like a bear, my arm arrives
at yours—oh, Honey, and we're back again,
me the Balboa, you the Darien,
lording the loud Pacific sands, our lives
as hazarded as when a petrel dives
to yank the dull sea's coverlet, or when,

breaking from me across the sand that's rink
and record of our weekend boning up
on *The Romantic Agony,* you sink
John Keats a good surf-fisher's cast out—plump
in the sun's wake—and the parched pages drink
that great whales' blanket party hump and hump.

GHOSTS OF THE MISSIONARIES

This is a quiet country. Chinamen
caress the fields with cultivators, groom
the streams with weirs. Mulberry bushes bloom
ultraconservatively. Now and then
the gang of blacks building a bridge say when,
and the weight falls *ker-pockk*. You can assume
the straw-thatch cottages, the paths. There's room
to do things in this land, there's room for men.

And as we walk, the barley fields comb to
behind us. Caucuses of crows take up
our cries. Gusts from a pasture pond renew
the early-morning vapors we drift through,
while cherry trees annunciate, *chirrup,*
the unsubstantiating dawn whereto.

CORA PUNCTUATED WITH STRAWBERRIES

Sandra and that boy that's going to get her in trouble
one of these days were out in the garden where anyone in
Mother's sickroom could see them out the upperleft corner of the
window sitting behind the garage feeding each other
blueberries and Cherry was helping with the dishes alone in the
kitchen and
um good strawberries if we did grow them just can't can without
popping one in every so often Henry was at it again in the
attic with that whatchamacallit of his when the Big
Bomb fell smack in the MacDonalds' yard you know over on
Elm and they got into Life and the papers and all all very
well but they might have been in when it hit and it would have
been a very different story for Lucy MacDonald then I'll tell
you well they say it was right in the Geographic Center of the
country the Geographic
woody Center you could hear it just as plain I thought the
elevator had blown up and I guess you read yourself the awful
things it would have
ak another one woody I tell you I don't know what's got
into these strawberries used to be so juicy they
say they only had the one and it's all it would have took well I
always knew we could beat the enemy they made such
shoddy tricks and spring-toys and puzzles and fuses and
things and besides, it wouldn't have been right.

COLD-WAR BULLETIN FROM THE CULTURAL FRONT

The proposed new U.S. Consulate at Algiers will be an ultra-modern structure . . . described by the architects as "a feast of great low glass domes."

We're building a building
in functional glass
at Algiers in Algeria:
no gargoyles, no gilding,
none of your crass
classic criteria:
one functional mass
of glass—

glass fibre, glass block,
glass fenestration,
with cut-glass tears
on the chandeliers
and pier-glass piers
clear to bedrock
(not far at Algiers)
for foundation.

But if domes of glass
of critical area
tend to let pass
units of mass,
heat, or hysteria,
we can gild with gilding
our functional building
in Algeria:

sun will not pierce
a glare so fierce,
and we'll station stations
of heads-of-legation
all round the block
with anti-rock rocks
(and anti-jeer jeers)
at Algiers.

UNWRAPPING THE IDOLS:
OFFICE OF THE EXHIBITION

Lady, this ritual object
I gently raise from its wrappings
into the welcomeless lighting
our elegant office affords it
springs from the limitless forest
our forefathers tailored away
from the edge of the map of their knowledge
till only the edge held sway.

Say once it was black as the raven,
its rites a daily observance
and every grove its altar;
say now it is private and pallid;
yet fingers like black wing-feathers
frightened to flight should raise it;
trees should lean heavy as temples;
walls and words should avoid it.

Time has its day: this object
cannot refashion its terror,
cannot remadden its lovers.
Taste of the jaded romantic
gives it a certain market
here where we see it emergent
out of its thick brown wrapping,
out of its white cloth swaddling.

Is it absurd to imagine
ancestral savages sent it
sailing its grave—a time-capsule
freighting through decadent ages
lost technological wonders
of body, of soul, of the dance—
as if there inhered in the shuttle
the work of a dark-limbed loom?

We weave here no such fabric,
barely contrive stiff gestures
of lumber and iron to clothe us;
and this, that compels a silence
hardly of awe or wonder,
mostly of indecision—
Lady, if this perplexes,
perhaps we might open that other . . .

WAR STORY

The 4th of July he stormed a nest.
He won a ribbon but lost his chest.
We threw his arms across the rest
 And kneed him in the chin.
 (You knee them in the chin
 To drive the dog-tag in.)

The 5th of July the Chaplain wrote.
It wasn't much; I needn't quote.
The widow lay on her davenport
 Letting the news sink in.
 (Since April she had been
 Letting the news sink in.)

The 6th of July the Captain stank.
They had us pinned from either flank.
With all respect to the dead and rank
 We wished he was dug in.
 (I mean to save your skin
 It says to get dug in.)

The word when it came was three days old.
Lieutenant Jones brought marigolds,
The widow got out the Captain's Olds
 And took him for a spin.
 (A faster-than-ever spin:
 Down to the Lake, and in.)

ELEGY

O lovers cold on mountain drives
   O lovers warm in valleys
O bold loves where the sand flea lives
   O furtive loves in alleys,
featherbeds are dear but sex
   is cheap:
pull your dashboards tight about your necks
   and sleep.

Long are the midnights where the spotlight plays;
soft are the motors of the night patrols;
you love, you dream, you re-rehearse your days:
the boastings by the lockers in the halls,
the maps to where the war is on the walls.

You wish yourself in Canaan or in Carthage
pitching grenades around the sun-struck corners;
you hide behind your books the pulps of carnage
and flip a spitball at the front-bench mourner:
he also dreams of machs and afterburners.

And even those who twist them dream of knives,
and heroes seek their heroes in a book:
the wing-commander shuts his Plutarch's Lives,
the gob his Batman, thug his Captain Hook,
each with the Far Antilles in his look.

Only, where dreams converge, at impact, zero,
a counter-current takes its pulse, and runs
through troubled worlds of sleep, to you as hero;
and we in bombers, planting sudden suns
that teem upon the earth by megatons—

we in the furrows, spitting fire to windward,
eternally astonished that the wind
spits back—we happy multitude—we kindred
haunters of beaches, mountain drives and blind
alleys—remake the loves we left behind.

White is the flesh entangled in the steel,
thrusting against the dead accelerator:
the moon its timeless lacquer sheds on heel
and trampled skirt alike—on nymph and satyr:
sleep then, within our dream: you dream no greater.

But lovers wake, the spotlight swings,
    the crunch is on the gravel:
start it, gun it, give it wings,
    pull in your ears and travel:
the world is wide God knows, but sex
    is deep:
pull your dashboards tight about your necks
    and sleep.

THE YALE SERIES OF YOUNGER POETS, which is designed to provide a publishing medium for the first volumes of promising poets, is open to men and women under forty who have not previously had a book of verse published. The Editor of the Series selects the winning volume in the annual contest and writes a preface for it. Manuscripts are received between March 1 and May 1 only; they should be addressed to the Editor, Yale Series of Younger Poets, Yale University Press, New Haven, Connecticut. Rules of the contest will be sent upon request.

VOLUMES 48–50, 52–55 ARE IN PRINT